Clues
for
Real Life

The Classic
Wit & Wisdom of

NANCY
DREW

Meredith Books
1716 Locust Street
Des Moines, Iowa 50309–3023
meredithbooks.com

Compiled by Jennifer Fisher.
Editor: Stephanie Karpinske
Book Design: Doug Samuelson

Printed in the United States of America.

First Edition.
Library of Congress Control Number: 2007925126
ISBN: 978-0-696-23624-2

Whether you're battling everyday villains, dating mysterious men, or just shopping for a fashionable frock, a few good clues for life are just what the modern woman needs.

Contents

ATTENTION MYSTERY MAVENS!
Look for clues as you read through the book. Nancy wrote them on scraps of paper.
Use them to solve the mysterious message on page 172.

Chapter 1

Hidden Secrets:
The Evolution of Nancy Drew

Whether you're a product of the groovy 1970s, the Great Depression, or the rock-around-the-clock '50s, there's one childhood experience many people share: devouring a Nancy Drew mystery under the covers after bedtime. (Sneaking around for such a good cause seems like something Nancy would approve of after all.) Although Nancy's fashions, favorite catchphrases, and car of choice changed to keep up with the newest trends, certain things remain constant: This daring heroine is ever brave in the face of danger, as capable as the men in her life, and unafraid to be both feminine and smart.

Today you may take for granted that Nancy embodies the strong American female spirit. But when she burst upon the book-world scene in 1930, she was a pioneer. Women had recently earned the right to vote, and they aspired to excitement, new challenges, and an escape from a life of domesticity. Nancy and her mystery-solving adventures were a welcome breath of fresh air, and faster than Nancy could solve her next case, she took her rightful place as a truly modern role model.

The Mystery Behind Carolyn Keene

Nancy Drew's fictional world is jam-packed with baffling mysteries and conundrums, so it's entirely fitting that Nancy's creators were hidden behind the pen name "Carolyn Keene." For many years rumors ran rampant about the identity of the "real" Carolyn Keene. The truth was stranger than fiction: There was not one Carolyn Keene, but many—male and female ghostwriters.

Nancy Drew was the brainchild of book mogul Edward Stratemeyer, who founded the Stratemeyer Syndicate around 1905. Although most people don't recognize Stratemeyer's name, it's likely they've read many of the hundreds of books his syndicate produced, including well-loved series about The Bobbsey Twins, The Rover Boys, Tom Swift, The Outdoor Girls, Dorothy Dale, and Ruth Fielding.

Stratemeyer was a genius storyteller who never lacked new and exciting story ideas. But he didn't have time to write all of his stories himself. Hence the birth of his Stratemeyer Syndicate.

The syndicate hired ghostwriters who wrote using Stratemeyer's completed plots and outlines. The ghostwriters served several purposes: They ensured that Stratemeyer had an outlet for all his ideas. They allowed Stratemeyer to maintain a level of continuity with each series; even if he changed ghostwriters, children would happily think their favorite authors were hard at work turning out new volumes each year. Plus the publishing business was much more lucrative for a copyright owner (who received royalties) than a ghostwriter (who was paid only a flat fee).

Clues to the Past:
So many ghostwriters! The first 56 Nancy Drew books (also known as the classic series, 1930 to 1979) were written by eight different people, including one man, Walter Karig, who wrote volumes 8 to 10.

Nancy Drew was one of Stratemeyer's last—and most successful—projects. He died on May 10, 1930, just two weeks after the Nancy Drew Mystery Stories series debuted with a three-volume set that included *The Secret of the Old Clock*, *The Hidden Staircase*, and *The Bungalow Mystery*.

The Fan-Favorite Formula

Nancy Drew mysteries are one of the world's most successful franchises because every story sticks to a similar, guaranteed-to-thrill formula: Nancy stumbles upon a baffling mystery, whisks herself and her chums off to exciting locales in search of clues, and deals with the trickery of sneaky criminals. While sleuthing, Nancy matches wits with embezzlers, kidnappers, jewel thieves, forgers, and those who won't hesitate to leave her imprisoned in a dark, mysterious place to starve. This favorite gumshoe always attracts a lot of drama—kidnappings, fake telegrams, burglars, and various threats of bodily harm. In case after case, these cliff-hangers press readers to turn the pages quickly, anxious to find out just how Nancy uses her wits to outsmart the criminals and save herself, her friends, and the day. Fortunately all this stress will never give Nancy gray hair: She is an eternal teenager, never aging past 18.

Clues to the Past: Nancy Drew's original name was "Nan Drew."

The First Carolyn Keene: Mildred Wirt Benson

It's not surprising that it was strong female writers who molded Nancy Drew into an enduring American icon. And the original Carolyn Keene, Mildred Wirt Benson, influenced the Nancy Drew series most profoundly. Mildred was born in 1905 but had the single-minded drive of a 21st-century career gal. This country girl from Iowa jump-started her writing career at age 13. Her first piece, *The Courtesy*, was published in a 1919 issue of the children's magazine *St. Nicholas*. She wrote short stories to help pay her way through the University of Iowa where she graduated in just three years.

Stratemeyer recognized Mildred's budding talents and in 1926 hired her to write for his popular Ruth Fielding series, which Mildred had read as a child. But as soon as he had the idea for the Nancy Drew series, Stratemeyer knew Mildred would be a perfect ghostwriter. In Mildred's capable hands, Nancy Drew became a breakout sensation with her exciting adventures and independent attitude. Mildred penned the first seven Nancy Drew books, plus volumes 11 through 25 and volume 30.

Strong Women Keep Nancy Strong: Harriet Stratemeyer Adams

Stratemeyer didn't believe that his daughters, Harriet Stratemeyer Adams and Edna C. Stratemeyer, should work outside the home. Yet they were the ones who shattered long-held stereotypes about a woman's role in corporate America when they took over the reins of their father's Syndicate upon his death in 1930. In fact under the sisters' management, the Syndicate remained a publishing force until 1984, when it was sold to Simon & Schuster.

Harriet, who was born in 1892 and studied writing at Wellesley College, had a particular fondness for Nancy Drew. After hiring several of what she considered unsatisfactory ghostwriters on volumes 26 through 29, Harriet began to write the Nancy Drew books herself, trying out her skills on volume 31. She tried a ghostwriter for volume 32 and again was not happy with the result. So from volume 33 on, Harriet decided to just write all of the books herself, which she did up until volume 56, the last book of the classic series. Harriet put her own stamp on Nancy's personality, transforming her into a cultured, finishing school girl with a personality that was more subdued and refined than it had been in the past. Harriet's philosophy was the Wellesley motto "Non ministrari sed ministrare"—which means "Not to be ministered unto but to minister"—and she felt that Nancy should embody this ideal.

Revisions, Revisions

If you compare the original texts of many Nancy Drew mysteries with later versions, you'll notice that often the stories are quite different. To provide a faster-paced read, the publishers shortened each of the first 34 volumes from 25 chapters to 20 chapters. These new revisions also removed language that reinforced ethnic stereotypes, although some readers felt these revisions also weakened the story detail and plot lines of the originals. Eight of the originals became all-new stories in the revising process: volumes 2, 4, 5, 11, 12, 14, 17, and 18 (for book titles, see series list, pages 20–21). The revisions also included many new cover illustrations.

Clues to the Past:
Happy birthday Nancy! In the 1950s, Nancy Drew magically aged from 16 to 18 to accommodate the driving laws in all states.

Check out the subtle—and not so subtle—differences between the original 1930 version of *The Secret of the Old Clock* and its 1959 revision.

	1930 original	**1959 revision**
Personality	Nancy Drew is plucky, brash, and opinionated.	Nancy becomes an unfailingly polite debutante type who's always dutiful.
Violence	On the trail of fleeing robbers, the shooter fired gunshots, blowing out a tire and causing the robbers to run into a ditch.	Violence is tamer. The criminals are bumbling, so gunfire isn't necessary.
The Bad Guys	The head robber is cruel, telling Nancy, "Now you can starve for all I care!"	A more sensitive robber tells Nancy, "Now you can spy all you want!"
	The villains are spied at the roadside inn "engaged in a drinking orgy."	The robbers are found "eating voraciously."
Breaking the Law	Nancy drives at "breathtaking speed."	Nancy drives "as rapidly as the law permitted."

Nancy Captures the Hearts of a Nation

Snooping for clues in old attics, chasing after suspects, and uncovering the schemes of impostors—Nancy Drew's adventures are exciting, imaginative thrill rides. But Nancy's enduring popularity lies not in the particulars of the mysteries she solved, but in the values and principles she stood for. Children of all ages identify with her independent spirit and ever-present curiosity. She is truly a trailblazer: This smart young woman has confidence and daring and crime-fighting abilities that set her apart from other book heroines. She'll be welcomed into American homes for many years to come.

By the Numbers

Nancy Drew went on to have many adventures—175 in all in the Nancy Drew Mystery Stories series and numerous spin-off series over the years. The last classic hardcover book was volume 56, The Thirteenth Pearl; *after that the books were issued in paperback. Today, there are more than 500 Nancy Drew mysteries, which include the classic series and many spin-off series and special volumes that have been printed, a testament to Nancy's longevity. Think you have Nancy's number? Check out these interesting history stats:*

4 Colors of Nancy's car (blue, maroon, yellow, and green)

2 Colors of Nancy's hair (blond and titian)

2 Number of Nancy's pets (Togo the dog and Snowball the cat)

10 Countries traveled to (Canada, Mexico, UK, France, Scotland, Kenya, Japan, Peru, Argentina, Turkey)

2 Number of times Ned Nickerson kidnapped

5 Number of Emerson College dances attended

6 Aliases used

8 Number of ghostwriters for classic Nancy Drew mysteries 1-56

56 Cases solved

1 Criminals who got away

Cover Girl: Our Favorite Fashionista

Nancy Drew fans dig the books' cover illustrations—and Nancy's ever-changing wardrobe—almost as much as the mysteries themselves. Can you match Nancy's fashion sensibilities with the appropriate artwork?

1930s: The Classy Sophisticate

At the very beginning of her crime-solving career, Nancy Drew was a blond-bobbed, all-American gal who favored cute cloche hats and fashionable, feminine frocks. On these covers Nancy was always illustrated in the midst of sleuthing. Commercial artist Russell H. Tandy was tapped to draw the first 26 Nancy Drew dust jackets (1930–1949) and page illustrations.

1950s: Bobby Socks and Scarves

As fashions changed, so did Nancy, and by the sock hop '50s, this teenager had a thing for circle skirts and thin-heel pumps. Illustrator William Sheldon Gillies, who drew new covers for volumes 27 through 29 (and revised volumes 1–9 and 11), often used his wife, Mary, as his model.

1960s: Demure Debutante

Nancy's look this decade included her quintessential flip hairdo, pantsuits, and sweater dresses, thanks to illustrator Rudy Nappi. As the series' longest running illustrator, Nappi illustrated books 30 through 56 and then went back and revised earlier covers.

1970s: Disco Mama

Yes, Nancy followed the fashion trends and in the '70s she donned bell-bottom pants. Hey, they were cool! Nappi continued to illustrate during these years. At this time the focus of the cover art shifted from a scenic portrayal of the books' action to images of Nancy with clues from the books.

25

How well do you know Nancy?

Beginner Sleuths

1. Where does Nancy live?
2. What is the name of Nancy's father?
3. Who is Nancy's boyfriend?
4. What is the original color of Nancy's car?
5. Who are Bess Marvin and George Fayne?
6. What kind of pet is Togo?
7. Name two of Nancy's favorite sleuthing tools.
8. Who is the Drews' housekeeper?
9. What is Nancy rewarded with at the end of *The Secret of the Old Clock*?
10. What college does Ned Nickerson attend?
11. In the revised books, how old was Nancy when her mom died?
12. Does Nancy Drew have a middle name?
13. What color was Nancy's hair originally?
14. In the first four books, who was Nancy's sleuthing chum?
15. How many books are in the classic hardcover series?

Answers: 1. River Heights 2. Carson Drew 3. Ned Nickerson 4. Blue 5. Best friends of Nancy Drew 6. Dog 7. Flashlight and magnifying glass 8. Hannah Gruen 9. Clock 10. Emerson 11. Three 12. No 13. Blond 14. Helen Corning 15. 56

Observant Sleuths

1. Name Nancy's cat.
2. What did Nancy Drew find in an old clock in *The Secret of the Old Clock*?
3. What kind of law practice did Carson Drew become famous for?
4. How old was Nancy when the series debuted back in 1930?
5. Name the two most prolific "Carolyn Keenes" who ghostwrote most of the first 56 volumes in the series.
6. Who created Nancy Drew?
7. On what date in 1930 did the first three Nancy Drew books debut?
8. What was the last Nancy Drew book to be issued with a dust jacket?
9. Who was the first actress to play Nancy Drew in the 1970s TV series on ABC?
10. In which book does Nancy Drew offer cooking advice and tips?

Answers: 1. Snowball 2. A notebook 3. Criminal law 4. 16 5. Mildred Wirt Benson and Harriet Stratemeyer Adams 6. Edward Stratemeyer 7. April 28, 1930 8. #38, *The Mystery of the Fire Dragon* 9. Pamela Sue Martin 10. *The Nancy Drew Cookbook*

Sophisticated Sleuths

1. What continent did Nancy travel to in #45, *The Spider Sapphire Mystery*?

2. In which book does Nancy follow a carrier pigeon?

3. What is Carson Drew's middle name?

4. In which book does Nancy use the alias Dru Gruen?

5. What caused Nancy Drew's mom's death?

6. In which book was Carson Drew kidnapped?

7. Nancy matches wits with villain Bushy Trott in which volume?

8. In which country does Nancy search for 99 steps?

9. Name the villain who got away in #8, *Nancy's Mysterious Letter*.

10. In which mystery does Nancy have a falling out with chums Bess and George?

Answers: 1. Africa 2. #10, *The Password to Larkspur Lane* 3. Campbell 4. #4, *The Mystery at Lilac Inn* 5. A long illness 6. #2, *The Hidden Staircase* 7. #21, *The Secret in the Old Attic* 8. France 9. Edgar Dixon 10. #9, *The Sign of the Twisted Candles*

How Did You Do?

All 35 = You're a Super Sleuth!

25-34 = You're a Real Nancy Drew Aficionado!

15-24 = You're Getting Warmer...

6-14 = Got Clues?

0-5 = Nancy Who?!

The Nancy Drew Mysteries Classic Hardcover Series

Volumes 1–56

1 THE SECRET OF THE OLD CLOCK
BY CAROLYN KEENE

2 THE HIDDEN STAIRCASE

3 THE BUNGALOW MYSTERY

4 The Mystery at Lilac Inn
CAROLYN KEENE

5 The Secret of Shadow Ranch
BY CAROLYN KEENE

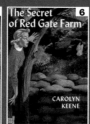
6 The Secret of Red Gate Farm
CAROLYN KEENE

7 The Clue in the Diary
CAROLYN KEENE

8 NANCY'S MYSTERIOUS LETTER
by CAROLYN KEENE

9 THE SIGN OF THE TWISTED CANDLES
CAROLYN KEENE

10 PASSWORD TO LARKSPUR LANE
by CAROLYN KEENE

11 The Clue of the Broken Locket
by CAROLYN KEENE

12 THE MESSAGE IN THE HOLLOW OAK
by CAROLYN KEENE

13 THE MYSTERY OF THE IVORY CHARM
by CAROLYN KEENE

14 THE WHISPERING STATUE
by CAROLYN KEENE

15 THE HAUNTED BRIDGE
by CAROLYN KEENE

16 THE CLUE OF THE TAPPING HEELS
by CAROLYN KEENE

17 MYSTERY OF THE BRASS-BOUND TRUNK

18 MYSTERY OF THE MOSS-COVERED MANSION
by CAROLYN KEENE

19 THE QUEST OF THE MISSING MAP
CAROLYN KEENE

20 THE CLUE IN THE JEWEL BOX
by CAROLYN KEENE

21 THE SECRET IN THE OLD ATTIC
by CAROLYN KEENE

22 THE CLUE IN THE CRUMBLING WALL
by CAROLYN KEENE

23 MYSTERY OF THE TOLLING BELL
by CAROLYN KEENE

24 THE CLUE IN THE OLD ALBUM
by CAROLYN KEENE

25 THE GHOST OF BLACKWOOD HALL
by CAROLYN KEENE

26 THE CLUE OF THE LEANING CHIMNEY
by CAROLYN KEENE

27 THE SECRET OF THE WOODEN LADY
by CAROLYN KEENE

 **28** THE CLUE OF THE BLACK KEYS

 **29** MYSTERY AT THE SKI JUMP

 **30** THE CLUE OF THE VELVET MASK

 **31** THE RINGMASTER'S SECRET *by CAROLYN KEENE*

 **32** THE SCARLET SLIPPER MYSTERY *by CAROLYN KEENE*

 **33** THE WITCH TREE SYMBOL *by CAROLYN KEENE*

 **34** THE HIDDEN WINDOW MYSTERY *by CAROLYN KEENE*

 **35** The Haunted Showboat

 **36** The Secret of the Golden Pavilion *by CAROLYN KEENE*

37 The Clue in the Old Stagecoach *by CAROLYN KEENE*

 **38** The Mystery of the Fire Dragon *by CAROLYN KEENE*

 **39** The Clue of the Dancing Puppet *by CAROLYN KEENE*

 **40** The Moonstone Castle Mystery *by CAROLYN KEENE*

 **41** The Clue of the Whistling Bagpipes *by CAROLYN KEENE*

 **42** The Phantom of Pine Hill *by CAROLYN KEENE*

 **43** THE MYSTERY OF THE 99 STEPS *by CAROLYN KEENE*

 **44** THE CLUE IN THE CROSSWORD CIPHER *by CAROLYN KEENE*

 **45** THE SPIDER SAPPHIRE MYSTERY

 **46** THE INVISIBLE INTRUDER *by CAROLYN KEENE*

 **47** THE MYSTERIOUS MANNEQUIN *by CAROLYN KEENE*

 **48** THE CROOKED BANISTER *by CAROLYN KEENE*

 **49** THE SECRET OF MIRROR BAY *by CAROLYN KEENE*

 **50** THE DOUBLE JINX MYSTERY *by CAROLYN KEENE*

 **51** MYSTERY OF THE GLOWING EYE *by CAROLYN KEENE*

 **52** THE SECRET OF THE FORGOTTEN CITY *by CAROLYN KEENE*

 **53** THE SKY PHANTOM *by CAROLYN KEENE*

 **54** THE STRANGE MESSAGE IN THE PARCHMENT *by CAROLYN KEENE*

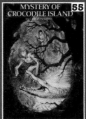 **55** MYSTERY OF CROCODILE ISLAND *by CAROLYN KEENE*

 **56** THE THIRTEENTH PEARL *by CAROLYN KEENE*

 *Chapter 2*

Career Clues:
Being Your Best on the Job

Nancy Drew can be counted among America's most talented female entrepreneurs after all she runs her own mystery-solving business that boasts an astounding 100 percent success rate! That's a job performance everyone would love to duplicate.

Nancy always knew she wouldn't hold a traditional office job. When solving *The Clue of the Dancing Puppet*, Nancy makes it clear that she prefers the freedom of independence to a regular 9 to 5 schedule. So instead Nancy's roadster is her office, whisking her off to interview suspects and search for clues. Sleuthing is her true passion, which is why she's at her best and brightest—and her happiest—when she's creating clever new ruses to foil the thieves, tailing suspects, or snooping around the criminal element.

It's no mystery, however, as to why Nancy has maintained her successful career: hard work, a willingness to learn from her mistakes, lots of support from her friends, and an insatiable appetite for all things mysterious.

When you're unusually good at what you do, the police will yearn for your women's intuition!

The Clue of the Leaning Chimney

Learn as You Go

When Nancy started sleuthing, there weren't classes she could enroll in to learn how to decipher mysterious codes or escape from a castle tower. So she perfected her skills on the job as each ghoulish riddle came along. It's a good thing that this brainy detective is always up for new challenges: She's able to fit in with the grace of a socialite and yet can vault fences and change flat tires with the ease of a tomboy. Perhaps the most important lesson Nancy's learned is one everyone should remember: Don't ignore your women's intuition. It will never fail you.

Selling charity tickets makes a great ruse to snoop in someone's house!

The Secret of the Old Clock

Bushes make a clever screen while you eavesdrop on unsuspecting suspects.

The Secret of the Old Clock

Where there's a hidden treasure and a phantom horse, there's probably some trickery going on!

The Secret of Shadow Ranch

If someone's trying to buy a house and it suddenly becomes haunted, it's probably not a coincidence.

The Hidden Staircase

Goblets on lower window sashes make great burglar alarms!

The Sign of the Twisted Candles

Knowing ventriloquism can help you make a dramatic entrance!

The Ringmaster's Secret

After being kidnapped, it's only proper to take a bath and change your clothes before reporting the crime to the police!

The Ghost of Blackwood Hall

It's polite to make purchases in shops where you're questioning the owner for clues.

The Strange Message in the Parchment

Count on Your Coworkers

When you run into a particularly sticky problem at work, you probably head to a coworker or boss to brainstorm new, creative solutions. That's true even if your problems are of the ghostly type! When the chips are down, Nancy can always rely on the help of her unofficial coworkers—chums Bess, George, and Helen; her motherly housekeeper Hannah Gruen; and special friends like Ned Nickerson. Nancy's pals are guaranteed to offer up their own unique ideas for acquiring clues and trapping suspects. Even the criminals (and in one instance a very talkative parrot) sometimes unwittingly help Nancy wrap up her cases.

When accused of crimes you didn't commit, name dropping your famous attorney father in your defense never hurts!

The Secret of Red Gate Farm

There's safety in numbers, especially when they're men!

The Haunted Showboat

If a parrot exclaims, "Go away. Danger," you might want to heed his advice!

The Mystery of the Moss-Covered Mansion

No matter how intent you are in solving a case, if your hostess wishes to have fun, better defer to her wishes.

The Password to Larkspur Lane

If you employ a dizzy maid who is scared of prowlers, you might just find yourself barricaded out of your home!

The Password to Larkspur Lane

Quick wits and good reflexes can save your chums in need when they've passed out from knockout spray!

The Phantom of Pine Hill

A special birdcall signal helps further secret communications among you and your chums when sleuthing outdoors in the midst of nefarious types.

The Mystery of the 99 Steps, The Double Jinx Mystery

Siccing your judo-obsessed chum on a fake police detective can produce gleeful results!

The Clue in the Crossword Cipher

When your friend suggests wearing disguises and you fail to heed her advice, receiving a threatening call that you're not who you say you are might make you feel a bit silly!

Mystery of Crocodile Island

Letting your chums carry duplicate keys to your car in case of emergency is great until you need your car and it's gone!

The Secret of Mirror Bay

20

Turn Mistakes into Lessons

Everyone makes mistakes on the job, but for Nancy those mistakes can be disastrous—and even fatal! Nancy is prone to be emotional and impulsive by nature, so she often faces danger without proper reinforcements—and that leads to many hard-learned lessons. But she is smart and learns quickly. Once she does something wrong, she never makes that same mistake twice. It's why her sleuthing skills improved every day—and why Nancy is the go-to girl when you need to capture the criminals fast and save the day!

If you find your name spelled in code in a "personal" ad placed by nefarious types, someone's probably on to you!

The Mystery of the Moss-Covered Mansion

Keeping an emergency five dollars in your purse is a great idea—until your purse is stolen!

The Mystery at the Ski Jump

Be sure to enunciate your name well when interviewing witnesses, or they might mistake you for their thieving maid Nanny Dew!

The Clue in the Old Album

A lesson learned from criminals—it never pays to flimflam the public!

The Ghost of Blackwood Hall

Disguising yourself with a different hairstyle might not cut it when you find yourself trapped in a villain's clutches …

The Clue of the Velvet Mask

When being followed, pretend to drop your purse and turn slightly for a more natural look-see!

The Clue in the Crumbling Wall

If you're planning to investigate a dark spooky attic, you might want to bring extra batteries for your flashlight.

The Hidden Staircase

Beware of who you give autographs to—your signature might later be used to forge checks.

The Clue of the Whistling Bagpipes

5

Posing under empty picture frames to elude a villain is a risky venture!

The Whispering Statue

Ignoring the strong smell of kerosene while investigating a criminal's hideout could lead to a hasty departure out a window on sheets!

The Scarlet Slipper Mystery

Using transparent aliases like "Nan Drewry" and "Edward Nickson" might just get you locked in a hallway!

The Thirteenth Pearl

Nancy's Resume

If Nancy needed to apply for a job, she would certainly have an interesting resume. Here is what she keeps on file— just in case an interesting job offer comes her way.

Nancy Drew
911 Drew Place
River Heights, U.S.A.
Home phone: 911-4SL-EUTH nancydrew@nancydrewdetectiveagency.com

OBJECTIVE
To solve mysteries and right wrongs. There's nothing that brings me more satisfaction than outwitting criminals and helping others!

SKILLS AND ABILITIES

Eavesdropping—through bushes, windows, you name it! No barrier is too great for my sleuth-worthy ears!

Finding Clues—I can sniff them out in two shakes.

Tailing Suspects—I drive as fast as the law will allow—with minor exceptions.

Interrogating Criminals and Witnesses— My persuasive powers and good negotiating skills are a criminal's undoing.

Deducing and Testing— I'm a logical thinker who is able to experiment with how it could have happened.

ADDITIONAL TALENTS

Mystery magnet—natural talent for unearthing unsolved mysteries

Extensive experience with magnifying glasses, flashlights, lock-picking essentials, hairpins, and many other devices

Able to identify footprints, fingerprints, tire marks, secret passageways, and hidden rooms

Fluent in handwriting analysis, foreign languages, women's intuition, disguises, aliases, and codes

Expert in finding lost objects and missing persons: wills, heirs, treasures, hidden objects

PROFESSIONAL HISTORY—FAMOUS CASES SOLVED
The Secret of the Old Clock—found lost will and showed up snooty Tophams
The Secret of Red Gate Farm—foiled a gang of counterfeiters masquerading as cultists
The Clue in the Jewel Box—found a queen's lost heir and thwarted an impostor
The Haunted Showboat—foiled "ghosts" haunting a showboat and recovered a treasure
The Thirteenth Pearl—busted up a ring of international jewel thieves posing as "pearl cultists"

EDUCATION
River Heights High School

SALARY REQUIREMENTS
An amateur sleuth never takes money as a reward—the reward for me is the fun I have solving mysteries and helping people!

Ever wonder what Nancy would do if she weren't a sleuth? Well, she's actually already tried out several careers so she could take her pick! Check out the many roles she has played.

Actress (*The Clue of the Dancing Puppet*)

Antique Dealer (*The Secret in the Old Attic*)

Archaeologist (*The Message in the Hollow Oak, The Clue in the Crossword Cipher, The Secret of the Forgotten City*)

Artist (*The Mystery of the Moss-Covered Mansion, The Quest of the Missing Map, The Hidden Window Mystery, The Double Jinx Mystery, The Strange Message in the Parchment*)

Attorney (learned law from her father Carson Drew; various volumes)

Bagpiper (*The Clue of the Whistling Bagpipes*)

Baker/Chef (*The Secret of Shadow Ranch, The Witch Tree Symbol*, various volumes)

Bomb Specialist (*The Haunted Showboat, The Double Jinx Mystery*)

Charity Fundraiser (*The Secret of the Old Clock, The Clue in the Leaning Chimney*)

Circus Trick Rider (*The Ringmaster's Secret*)

Dance Teacher (*The Scarlet Slipper Mystery*)

Diver (*The Mystery at Lilac Inn, The Phantom of Pine Hill, The Secret of Mirror Bay, The Secret of the Golden Pavilion*)

Engineer: Robotics (*The Crooked Banister*)

Florist (*The Password to Larkspur Lane*)

Gardener (*The Password to Larkspur Lane, The Clue in the Crumbling Wall*)

Ghost Tour Guide (*The Invisible Intruder*)

Lifeguard (*The Bungalow Mystery, The Password to Larkspur Lane, The Clue in the Jewel Box*)

Legal Assistant (various volumes)

Locksmith (various volumes)

Mechanic (*The Secret of the Old Clock*)

Model (*The Clue in the Jewel Box*)

Nurse (*The Secret of the Old Clock, The Haunted Bridge*, various volumes)

Pilot (*The Clue in the Crumbling Wall, The Sky Phantom*)

Professional Dancer (*The Secret of the Golden Pavilion, The Double Jinx Mystery*)

Professional Golfer (*The Haunted Bridge*)

Professional Ice Skater (*The Mystery at the Ski Jump*)

Professional Singer (*The Spider Sapphire Mystery*)

Professional Tap Dancer (*The Clue of the Tapping Heels*)

Promoter (*The Secret of Red Gate Farm*)

Psychologist (*The Secret of the Old Clock*)

Race Car Driver (various volumes)

Sailor (various volumes)

Seamstress (*The Secret of Red Gate Farm*)

Sprinter (various volumes)

Translator (*The Clue in the Crumbling Wall, The Mystery of the Tolling Bell*)

Treasure Hunter (*The Secret of Shadow Ranch, The Message in the Hollow Oak, The Quest of the Missing Map, The Clue of the Black Keys, The Haunted Showboat*)

Veterinarian (*The Witch Tree Symbol*)

Waitress (*The Mystery of the Tolling Bell*)

Chapter 3

Friendship Files: Lessons Learned from Bess and George

Best friends are like high heels: Every girl needs a good pair! Nancy Drew palled around with Helen Corning until she met cousins Bess Marvin and George Fayne—now solving mysteries is always more fun with these two chums! This loyal duo gladly chooses mystery solving over the cute boy who asked them out on a date, doesn't criticize Nancy's choice of job (even though it's dangerous!), and is always up for grabbing a late-night snack. George and Bess have completely opposite personalities and are like oil and water when they're in the same room. George is brave and bold and always up for new thrills and spooky chills. Although Bess is more timid and often scared (or starving for a comforting bite), she always comes through for Nancy at the perfect moment. Despite their differences, this trio's friendship remains tried and true.

You know you've got a loyal friend when she postpones a date three times to sleuth with you!

The Clue in the Diary

Find Friends You Can Trust

True friends are ones who stick with you through good times and bad. Nancy's friends George and Bess have been kidnapped, bound, left to starve, and knocked unconscious—and yet they rebound from each bone-chilling adventure without a complaint, ready to help bring another criminal to justice. For Nancy, a true friend is one who will walk down dark alleys, sleuth in haunted houses, and risk life and limb for a good clue!

When you've been accused of passing a counterfeit bill, it helps to have friends with extra cash to help cover your bill.

The Secret of Red Gate Farm

When lost in the mountains, try to put on a brave front for morale's sake.

The Secret of Shadow Ranch

18

You know your friends are loyal when they'll sleep in the garage to help catch a thief.

The Clue of the Tapping Heels

When your chum goes undercover, a nice set of calling cards with her alias makes a nice gift.

The Whispering Statue

Using rope tricks you learned at Shadow Ranch can come in handy when rescuing a sleepwalking chum from falling off a fire escape.

The Message in the Hollow Oak

Bound and gagged on a train to nowhere really makes you appreciate your chums.

The Ringmaster's Secret

You can always talk a loyal friend into joining you in your schemes and ruses.

The Password to Larkspur Lane

Sleuthing for your friend can get you covered in gobs of glue and ink!

The Double Jinx Mystery

9

Accept Differences in Your Friends

When faced with life's big decisions—Should I take that new job? Should I say "yes" to his proposal?—most people ask several different friends for advice. That's because each friend brings a unique perspective to the situation. When faced with life's mysteries, Nancy Drew is happy to have friends with polar-opposite personalities helping her. Bess is timid, so she's often happy to let Nancy and George charge ahead while she stays behind and serves as a lookout. Nancy prides herself on being a subtle sleuth, so having a blunt and brazen chum like George has its own rewards—and George's judo skills never fail to come in handy!

When your chums start to bicker, you can always diffuse the situation by changing the subject to less stressing topics—like counterfeiters and thieves.

The Secret of Red Gate Farm

Remember, it's OK if your chum prefers things which don't smack of mystery.

The Haunted Bridge

When you become stranded because your clothes have been stolen, you might be frustrated at your chum who's wandered off, until you learn of her being locked in a tower.

The Clue in the Crumbling Wall

If your chum is a natural born gossip, you learn to sleuth more sneakily around her sometimes.

The Hidden Staircase

If you make a bet with your friends, you might end up knitting a sweater when you're proved wrong.

The Clue in the Old Stagecoach

Be careful around your klutzy friends, you might get dragged over a cliff!

The Secret of the Golden Pavilion

Spoilsports are often left as guards on sleuthing missions.

The Mystery of the 99 Steps

It's great when your wisecracking chum can make an awful situation seem funny.

The Phantom of Pine Hill

When you're known for being the athletic one in the group, you might be asked to be the first to test the makeshift sheet-rope escape out of a burning house.

The Scarlet Slipper Mystery

Sometimes you need to take a break from staking out counterfeiters for a festive round of croquet and horseshoes.

The Secret of Red Gate Farm

A tennis match is a great way to unwind after days of sleuthing.

The Mysterious Mannequin

Attending concerts can lead to showcasing your talent for singing in Swahili.

The Spider Sapphire Mystery

You can have a humorous and sparkling conversation without any mention of crooks and clues!

The Haunted Showboat

Sightseeing in the French Quarter in New Orleans is a lot of fun and a great way to break up sleuthing adventures.

The Haunted Showboat

5

Touring a bagpipe factory can be quite entertaining as well as educational.

The Clue of the Whistling Bagpipes

When snowed in from sleuthing, throwing a masquerade party just might get you three cheers!

Nancy's Mysterious Letter

There's nothing better than when your friend surprises you with delicious cakes and pies.

Nancy's Mysterious Letter

It's fun to take five from sleuthing for a little swim and a rousing diving contest.

The Password to Larkspur Lane

Friend or Foe? How do you know?

When you're just getting to know someone, how do you know if they are a loyal pal or a backstabbing enemy? Nancy would tell you to first gather some clues from their behavior and then come to a conclusion. Below is a list of some telling behaviors. Think of the person you're wondering about, then answer yes or no based on whether or not this person engages in the following behaviors.

1. Shadows you around town while trying to stay hidden in the scenery.
   ☐ Y ☐ N

2. Looks forward to every exciting new adventure.
   ☐ Y ☐ N

3. Writes threatening notes to you.
   ☐ Y ☐ N

4. Takes your car—and never returns it.
   ☐ Y ☐ N

5. Worries about your safety and asks you to give up detective work for less dangerous pursuits.
   ☐ Y ☐ N

6. Drags you unwillingly to places you don't want to go.
   ☐ Y ☐ N

7. Loves to share a good snack.
   ☐ Y ☐ N

8. Irritates you so much that you're tempted to utter a snarky retort.
   ☐ Y ☐ N

9. Wears disguises when it's not Halloween.
   ☐ Y ☐ N

10. Has a highly unusual name that seems more like an alias meant to hide his or her true identity.
   ☐ Y ☐ N

If you answered YES to 1, 3, 4, 6, 8, 9, 10: This person is probably a foe!

If you answered YES to 2, 5, or 7: This person is probably a friend.

If you STILL aren't sure, keep watching this person's behavior for more clues!

Personality Match: Are you like Nancy, Bess, or George?

Which of these adventures is right up your alley?
1. Staking out suspects and eavesdropping
2. Hitting the sales at the mall
3. Running in a marathon

While visiting your eccentric aunt, you stumble upon a secret passageway in her attic. What do you do?
1. Explore it, hoping you stumble upon something mysterious
2. Run screaming at the first sign of insects or mice
3. Hope there's a sneaky sort hiding out, so you can try out your latest judo trick

What's your favorite weekend activity?
1. Multitasking on your many ongoing projects
2. Going to the spa
3. Mountain biking

A friend calls with boyfriend troubles. What advice do you give?
1. Follow him; he might secretly be seeing someone else.
2. Cook for him. A way to a man's heart is through his stomach!
3. Go for a jog; it often clears one's mind of troubles.

When a man flirts with you, what do you do?
1. Feel a rush of excitement, then wonder if he's got any skeletons in his closet
2. Flirt right back
3. Wonder if he'd make a nice sparring partner at the gym

A friend laments that she's going on a diet. What is your response?
1. Support her decision and offer helpful advice
2. Offer to join her, after you finish your triple-fudge brownie sundae!
3. Tease and nag her when she overindulges

How Did You Do?

Mostly 1s = You're an observant detective like Nancy!

Mostly 2s = Like Bess, food and boys are right up your alley!

Mostly 3s = Athletics is your true passion, just like George!

Chapter 4

Mysterious Men:
Solving Your Dating Dilemmas

Face it: The average gal meets many Mr. Wrongs on her search for Mr. Right. Nancy Drew is no exception. She flirts with danger on a daily basis, often in the form of dastardly villains, jewel thieves, and kidnappers. All that intrigue and time spent sniffing out clues takes its toll on Nancy's love life. But Nancy is lucky to have a very supportive (and patient!) boyfriend in Ned Nickerson, a college football player who loves to lend a hand with Nancy's detecting schemes. Like many career gals, Nancy doesn't worry about whether she and Ned will end up living happily ever after—her main life goals are to snoop, meddle, and get to the bottom of every baffling mystery that crosses her path. Men can be a fun distraction, but mysterious affairs are timeless!

Do act mysterious, it always keeps them coming back for more!

Nancy's Mysterious Letter

Dating Dos and Don'ts

Rule No. 1: Your first love may be your work, but don't let your boyfriend know that! Nancy has learned the dos and don'ts of dating the hard way—by making lots of mistakes. But she knows that to keep her boyfriend Ned around, mystery and adventure must sometimes take a back seat to romance. This independent woman is not afraid to use her feminine charms, but she'll also put her date to work for her tracking down clues. And no matter who flirts with her, Nancy never forgets to let Ned know he's her special friend, lest she find herself dateless!

Don't make your date take another girl to a BBQ so you can go off sleuthing.

The Bungalow Mystery

Do be modest! Don't make yourself appear to be too perfect ...

Nancy's Mysterious Letter

Do stroke his ego every once in a while and ask for a little male assistance.

The Whispering Statue

Don't refuse a gift when a man wants to treat you!

The Mystery of the Tolling Bell

Don't have other steady dates, or your special friend might not forgive you as easily for all the scrapes you get him.

The Clue of the Tapping Heels

Do be a pretty sight for sore eyes.

The Mystery of the Moss-Covered Mansion

Don't assume he didn't want to ask you to a big dance; it might be that your rival waylaid his invitation to you!

The Secret in the Old Attic

Do nearly faint upon being rescued so you can be picked up and held by good strong arms.

The Secret in the Old Attic

19

Do let him take charge every once in a while—demanding your presence at a school dance isn't so bad.

The Secret in the Old Attic

Don't let him think you can always easily arrange your sleuthing around his social calendar.

The Mystery at the Ski Jump

Do try to focus on your boyfriend's conversation even though tales of football and insurance sales are not as exciting as sleuthing.

The Mysterious Mannequin

Find a Balance Between Career and Romance

Is your first love your career or your hunky escort to the social soiree? Nancy is often torn between those two passions, especially since mysteries have a way of finding her at the most inopportune times. Ned and Nancy's romantic dinners are often interrupted because of Nancy's one-track mind for clues. After all, that waiter might be a thief or that movie attendant could be a scam artist. But Nancy tries to give Ned the attention he deserves, listening (or at least pretending to listen) to his discussions of insurance sales and football games. This multitasking gumshoe knows that being observant in romance and mysteries is imperative.

Every once in a while, earn points by asking to be forgiven for mixing mysteries with fun!

Nancy's Mysterious Letter

Some men don't like to be kept waiting—even for a mystery!

The Hidden Staircase

Keep things flexible—you never know when you're asked out if a mystery might transpire!

The Sign of the Twisted Candles

Even though you'd like to dance with that young man, don't mix romance with detective work!

The Bungalow Mystery

Sometimes you have to be coaxed into giving up sleuthing to attend a dance.

The Mystery of the Ivory Charm

You can escape an unwanted suitor by leaving town to sleuth.

The Secret in the Old Attic

Though getting stuck at the top of a Ferris wheel can foil your sleuthing plans, it's a great excuse to enjoy some quality time with your boyfriend.

The Clue in the Jewel Box

2

When you're down in the dumps over a baffling case, being asked out on a date can be a real pick-me-up.

The Clue in the Old Album

Dream or Dud?
How to Tell He's a Keeper

Every relationship has clues as to whether it's the "forever" one or not. For you maybe it's important that he's good with animals or that he loves to ski. Nancy's criteria is a little different: Her dream guy, Ned, puts himself in harm's way to save her life, wrestles with villains, takes a punch or two for the team, and cheers her up when she's run out of clues. He's big and brawny and can handle the bad guys, so surely he's proved himself to be Nancy's Mr. Right!

When you stick your boyfriend in a cabin with a sick man and live high on the hog at a nearby resort, he might get a bit cranky, but if he complies, he might just be the man for you.

The Haunted Bridge

You know your father likes your date when he shakes his hand really heartily.

The Clue in the Diary

When getting a call from a guy makes you send your slippers flying to the nether regions of your bedroom, you might just be infatuated!

The Clue in the Diary

You know he's the guy for you when he's a tried and true friend.

The Whispering Statue

You know he's the right guy for you when he can dismantle a mad scientist's powerful transmitter and save the world!

Mystery of the Moss-Covered Mansion

When he wants to make a date with you to solve a mystery, you've got him wrapped around your fingers.

The Mystery of the Tolling Bell

You might just like a guy if an intense gaze from him causes you to blush to the roots of your hair in a glorious crimson flush!

The Secret in the Old Attic

When your boyfriend is chloroformed and tied to a tree and he's just disgusted with himself at being caught instead of you for getting him into this predicament, you know he likes you.

The Ghost of Blackwood Hall

When he's willing to risk getting another black eye just to be with you, he's the guy!

The Clue of the Velvet Mask

MYSTERIOUS MEN

Is Ned really right for Nancy? If Nancy and Ned each ran a personal ad, here's an idea of how it might appear. Looks like they really are a match!

Slim Sleuth Seeks Man of Mystery

Slim, attractive 18-year-old female amateur detective seeking tall, dark, and handsome guy who likes adventure. A loyal and intelligent guy who can brave criminals and rescue me when the chips are down is a plus! Must have a car in case mine breaks down or is tampered with. Must also be patient, a good dancer, and able to literally roll with the punches. My dream man has a serious, practical side but can also have fun. If you like sleuthing in the moonlight and hunting down villains in dark alleys, you're the guy for me!

Handsome College Student Seeks Adventuresome Gal

Multitalented, tall, dark, and handsome Emerson College student with intelligence, patience, and a sense of humor seeking slim and attractive female to be his lively companion, attend numerous fraternity dances, and take moonlit walks. Must like to help others. Must be willing to occasionally let me use my strong arms or football tackle maneuvers to keep you safe from harm. If you are a gal who likes adventure and is a bit mysterious, you're the one for me!

When Ned's not around ...

Every modern gal knows that you often can't count on a man to help you out of a difficult situation. You need to be strong and use your knowledge and skills to save yourself. When Ned and her friends aren't around, Nancy finds creative ways to get out of perilous predicaments. Try to match the situations below with Nancy's clever escape techniques.

1. Locked in temple by crazy astrologer
2. Bound in basement of bungalow
3. Found a bomb in her car
4. Bound and gagged in hayloft
5. Held captive on boat
6. Stuck with bottle of deadly sleeping potion
7. Accosted by masked men while in car
8. Almost grabbed by villain
9. Thrown in cistern
10. Locked in hallway

a. Uses scythe to break free
b. Uses ring of keys to unlock door
c. Uses sleeve as a stopper
d. Uses ladder pieces to dig out
e. Honks horn for help
f. Pretends to faint and slump
g. Uses special hand trick to escape
h. Turns the switch off
i. Jumps overboard and swims
j. Taps heels to attract a rescuer

Answers: 1.j, 2.g, 3.h, 4.a, 5.i, 6.c, 7.e, 8.f, 9.d, 10.b

 *Chapter 5*

Everyday Villains: Dealing with Difficult People

You have probably encountered people who try your patience—from annoying bosses and nosy coworkers to irritating sales clerks and bad drivers. For supersleuth Nancy Drew, dealing with threats, bad manners, and violent tempers is all in a day's work. After all thieves and racketeers will pull out every dirty trick in the book. Although she often has to bite back a snarky retort, Nancy is unfailingly polite because she knows she'll catch more bees with honey. When she's forced to deal with nefarious characters, she outsmarts them with a sweet smile and a determined frame of mind. Her motto? Keep your enemies close so you can keep a watchful eye on the mystery prize.

When people irritate you, it's best to stifle a snarky retort and not let them get the best of you.

The Secret of the Old Clock

Be Nice—Even When Others Aren't

Sometimes being a detective can make Nancy's blood boil—especially when she's bothered by a pestering fool, dealing with old fogies, or being falsely accused of something. No matter how difficult those snooty snobs or arrogant impostors make her life, Nancy keeps her chin up and stays on her best behavior. While most people would likely strike out at the offender, Nancy believes that it's important to stay calm, cool, and collected—even in the worst situations.

When someone's mother doesn't want you associating with her daughter because you're a detective, you should control your temper, but you can always sic your cat on them.

The Mystery of the Brass-Bound Trunk

If you're ever locked in a tack room, sometimes it's best to throw everyone off guard and ask who locked you in with a big sweet smile on your face.

The Secret of Shadow Ranch

It can be infuriating when you're accused of stealing someone's letter (from their good-for-nothing brother no less), but try to keep a level head and you can always remind them that it's illegal to send cash through the mail.

The Hidden Window Mystery

Even shrill old fogies who have poor impressions of young people can't get the best of you if you remain calm, and you might just find out a clue or two.

Nancy's Mysterious Letter

If a mean man tries to make amends for his poor behavior after he finds out you're a person of importance, you can always pretend not to notice his attempt to shake your hand.

Nancy's Mysterious Letter

Battle Boorish Behavior (and get what you want!)

Nancy may be polite, but she's certainly no pushover. She always gets her way—squeezing the information she needs from ill-tempered suspects—with patience, perseverance, and a few tricks of her own. The lesson here is that sometimes you have to finesse your way around the poor manners of louts and malcontents to get the job done! And when dealing with tricksters, that women's intuition often comes into play. Nancy has an uncanny ability to read people's behavior and figure out when they're lying or hiding an important clue—often turning the tables on them!

While you might be upset that a suspect has rudely thrown your sketch into the fireplace, secretly you are elated because you touched a nerve!

The Hidden Window Mystery

6

When a crook puts your car out of commission, you can always repay him the debt and do the same to his car!

The Mystery of the Moss-Covered Mansion

Always get the license number of pushy people wanting to buy clues to your mystery!

The Quest of the Missing Map

When you've been accused of causing one's undoing, sometimes a laugh and a smile is the best revenge!

The Secret of the Old Clock

When your father's new legal assistant tries to take over your case, watch out—two can play at that game!

Mystery of the Glowing Eye

Sometimes pretending to go into a trance and reveal secrets from the past can illicit a confession from even the most high-handed types.

The Mystery of the Ivory Charm

You can rile up a villain by pretending to throw a treasure off a cliff.

The Secret of Shadow Ranch

When a crazed villain leaps off and starts dancing with you across a field, take this opportunity to interrogate him for clues in between twirls!

The Double Jinx Mystery

When an angry shopkeeper won't let you purchase a book, those underlined words inside might be a code used in some nefarious plot!

The Mystery of the Fire Dragon

Don't Fret About a Threat

Do you ever encounter people who threaten you just because they think they can? Well the key to dealing with these menaces is to stand your ground. Just consider how Nancy deals with the many threats that come her way. Without this teen detective, the criminals would run the show. Nancy's got to let them know who's boss! She refuses to be intimidated by ominous notes, fake telegrams, or veiled threats from all sorts of schemers. She doesn't take any of the menacing warnings too seriously (especially the anonymous ones!)—in fact they just make her more determined to cut through the web of intrigue and hand the criminals over to the police!

When threatened with a hairbrush by a vicious woman, remain calm and speak in cold level tones.

The Sign of the Twisted Candles

A letter that tells you to give up your case or face worse harm just makes you want to sleuth harder!

The Spider Sapphire Mystery

There's nothing worse than a threatening note that demands you stay at home, when you're just not the stay-at-home kind of gal!

The Clue in the Old Album

An ominous message that reads 4 + 9=13 proves only one thing—criminals can count—but you're not fooled by their veiled threats!

The Thirteenth Pearl

Always remember, writers of anonymous notes are cowards!

The Scarlet Slipper Mystery

A warning to stay out of France just makes a girl want to take a risk!

The Mystery of the 99 Steps

A stuffed wryneck bird on the lawn is a sign that you might be jinxed!

The Double Jinx Mystery

A warning from someone who signs their note "The Phantom" can seem a bit comical.

The Phantom of Pine Hill

Match the Villain to the Crime

The shifty villains who Nancy Drew runs into are memorable because they often are caricatures: They sport spiffy names, wear suspiciously ill-fitting clothes that are several seasons out of style, and can't disguise their terrible scowls or the cruel glints in their eyes. But their outlandish attempts to foil Nancy won't keep them out of jail for long! Test your memory: Can you link these crooks to their crimes?

1. Mary Mason
2. Bullseye Bellows
3. Nitaka
4. Reinhold Kroon
5. Howard Brex
6. Luis Llosa, aka El Gato
7. Foxy Felix Raybolt
8. Jim O'Keefe, aka Tim O'Malley
9. Louis Aubert
10. Mitzi Channing
11. Grumper
12. Edgar Dixon
13. Benny the Slippery One Caputti
14. Swahili Joe
15. Bushy Trott

a. sheet music thief
b. inheritance thief
c. fake alchemist and financial crook
d. lonely hearts club mail scammer
e. cosmetic company scammer
f. stock swindler
g. diamond thief
h. séance racketeer
i. strong-arm man and kidnapper
j. jewel thief
k. treasure thief
l. drug smuggler
m. patent swindler
n. thieving Double Scorps Gang leader
o. doll thief

Answers: 1. g, 2. k, 3. o, 4. b, 5. h, 6. l, 7. m, 8. n, 9. c, 10. f, 11. e, 12. d, 13. j, 14. i, 15. a

If you want to read the stories that featured these villains, here are the corresponding book titles.

1. *The Mystery at Lilac Inn*
2. *The Quest of the Missing Map*
3. *The Clue in the Old Album*
4. *The Ringmaster's Secret*
5. *The Ghost of Blackwood Hall*
6. *The Clue in the Crossword Cipher*
7. *The Clue in the Diary*
8. *The Secret of the Golden Pavilion*
9. *The Mystery of the 99 Steps*
10. *The Mystery at the Ski Jump*
11. *The Mystery of the Tolling Bell*
12. *Nancy's Mysterious Letter*
13. *The Thirteenth Pearl*
14. *The Spider Sapphire Mystery*
15. *The Secret in the Old Attic*

Everyday Villains

Difficult people lurk almost everywhere you go—at restaurants, online, on trips. So how do you handle these people without losing your cool? Act like Nancy. Take this quiz and see if you can predict how Nancy would deal with these everyday villains.

1. **If stuck in a traffic jam surrounded by irate drivers while chasing down a clue, Nancy would ...**
   a) Honk her horn repeatedly while yelling at fellow drivers out of her car window
   b) Remain patient and daydream about clues
   c) Call Bess on her cell phone and gossip about the latest celebrity tabloid story

2. **If a mean trickster left Nancy and her friends in the woods, Nancy would ...**
   a) Remind them to hug a tree and stay put for eventual rescue
   b) Find suitable shelter and whip up a nourishing meal from available vegetation
   c) Feel like a failure—supersleuths aren't supposed to get lost

3. **If a villain slashed Nancy's tires and left her stranded on a deserted road late at night, Nancy would ...**
   a) Wait to be rescued—hopefully by friends and not foes
   b) Fix the flat with ease and go on her merry way
   c) Bemoan the fact that her cell phone doesn't have a signal to call for help

4. **If a mysterious, masked stranger refused to reveal his identity after being asked repeatedly, Nancy would ...**
   a) Yell at him to leave her alone
   b) Boldly grab his mask off and reveal his true identity
   c) Play guessing games until she figured out who he was

5. **If Nancy found out someone was hacking into her email account, she would ...**
   a) Discover their identity and inundate them with spam
   b) Trace them to a specified location and have Chief McGinnis pick them up for questioning
   c) Create emails crazy enough to scare them away from any more hacking

6. **If Nancy were waiting for an important phone call and received an annoying sales call instead, she would ...**
   a) Hang up
   b) Politely listen to the salesman's pitch and then simply say no thank you
   c) Order away

7. **If she discovered that nosy neighbors had been snooping around her house while she was out, Nancy would ...**
   a) Put up a "No Trespassing" sign
   b) Snoop around their place for clues— they've probably got something to hide
   c) Move to an isolated area without annoying, pesky neighbors

How Did You Do?

Mostly a's = Nancy Drew was never this realistic!

Mostly b's = You know your Nancy Drew!

Mostly c's = You might benefit from reading a few of Nancy Drew's mysteries!

Chapter 6

The Traveling Suitcase: Around the World with Nancy

Nancy Drew's passport can turn even the most well-traveled green with envy: It's filled with stamps from Argentina, Kenya, Hong Kong, Turkey, Mexico, and scores of other exotic locales. Nancy's prowess as a sleuth makes her a global force to be reckoned with as she travels far and wide in search of clues and dastardly villains. But no matter whether Nancy is traveling overseas or crisscrossing the U.S., she is sure to pack enough pluck and resolve (and maybe a few handy disguises) to tackle any puzzler thrown her way. And mystery follows her wherever she travels! This independent, all-American adventurer tracks down suspects in New Orleans, enjoys an African safari while tailing jewel thieves—and still has time to shop for souvenirs!

You know you're clues-obsessed when you can't imagine a vacation without a mystery to solve.

The Mystery of the Brass-Bound Trunk

The Fun (and Mystery) of Travel

Even though she loves her work, Nancy believes that everyone needs a little time away to relax and explore new places. Like many people, Nancy makes sure her vacations include plenty of time for sightseeing, sampling the local fare, and taking in the historical sights. Unfortunately villains are often hot on her trail, making relaxation a tad difficult. But this supersleuth meets every challenge head-on. She forges a raging Arizona river on horseback, sleuths at night in the twisted, tangled Louisiana bayous, and takes a near plunge down a volcano's crater in Hawaii. It may not be a day at the beach, but extreme vacations are much more fitting for Nancy. You can learn a lot of traveling tips and tricks from this clever gumshoe!

When traveling by car, always check for car bombs and other signs of tampering.

The Haunted Showboat

Be careful when sightseeing around volcano craters, you might just take the plunge!

The Secret of the Golden Pavilion

A spiffy yellow roadster is great for traveling—but might make you rather conspicuous to villains on your tail.

The Haunted Showboat

Tenderfoot sleuths traveling in the Southwest will soon learn one way or the other to become water-conscious Westerners.

The Secret of Shadow Ranch

A visit to a historical museum can lead to clues in old Valentines.

The Secret of Mirror Bay

While sightseeing in a place like Pirate's Alley, you're bound to run into that thief you're looking for!

The Haunted Showboat

It's fun to multitask and solve local mysteries while traveling—like the sinking of a ship many years before or digging up an old treasure!

Mystery of Crocodile Island

When traveling in search of an old-time bandit's hideout, you're sure to find a villain lurking!

The Secret of the Forgotten City

When Abroad, Do as the Locals Do

Most overseas travelers try their best to avoid looking like tourists lest they become the easy targets of crooks and pickpockets. Nancy is no different. She wants to evade the crooks who are seeking to foil her every move so that she can solve the case. This global traveler has learned many tricks for blending in with the locals. She moves through town without detection by using the local lingo, chatting in various dialects, dressing in traditional clothes, and respecting ancient customs. By following Nancy's lead, you're sure to travel in foreign lands with ease—until that pesky villain catches up with you!

Dressing like a local Spanish dancer makes a nice cover to gain information from nefarious types!

The Clue in the Crossword Cipher

When traveling, sample the local menu fare!

The Secret of the Golden Pavilion

Sampling too much local fare can lead to an unpleasant tummy ache!

The Clue in the Crossword Cipher

Dining with the natives and astounding them with your ability to sing in Swahili will earn you a good meal.

The Spider Sapphire Mystery

While sleuthing at Versailles, you might end up in Louis XIV's bed!

The Mystery of the 99 Steps

When warned by a cantankerous Monsieur Neuf to stay out of France, indulge his threats and go to France anyway!

The Mystery of the 99 Steps

While traveling in Scotland, blend in with a family tartan.

The Clue of the Whistling Bagpipes

Do your part—when a bagpiping villain is arrested, take his place on Ben Nevis to musically draw out the rest of his gang.

The Clue of the Whistling Bagpipes

Traveling in Mexico helps you learn Mexican dialects which are sure to be handy in future mystery solving ventures.

The Secret of the Forgotten City

Explore local customs by getting yourself invited to a Japanese wedding.

The Thirteenth Pearl

Always Get a Souvenir

After you've returned home from exploring new lands and cultures, it's nice to have a memento of your thrilling adventures. After all a great souvenir can help you remember fondly the time you were lost in the wilderness, knocked unconscious in an old haunted showboat, or nearly blown out of a plane over Peru. Or if a mystery later ensues, your special token may just be a clue! So when traveling near or far, always remember to stop in at the local tourist shops and bazaars.

A turquoise pillbox is a nice reminder of a Southwestern vacation!

The Secret of Shadow Ranch

Pieces of eight necklaces and pins make mysterious souvenirs!

The Mystery of the Moss-Covered Mansion

Pralines and pecan nougat make really delicious souvenirs.

The Haunted Showboat

Pearl jewelry souvenirs will remind your friends and family of the time you nabbed those crazy pearl cultists!

The Thirteenth Pearl

Always remember your aunt when shopping for souvenirs.

The Secret of the Golden Pavilion

Nothing says France like a musical teapot.

The Mystery of the 99 Steps

An African death mask in your likeness might sound a bit morbid until you find out the eye sockets can secrete hidden objects!

The Spider Sapphire Mystery

5

Where in the World Is Nancy?

Wherever Nancy traveled,
a mystery was never far behind.
Match these travel locations to
the mystery that Nancy solved there.

1. The Secret of Shadow Ranch

2. The Clue in the Crossword Cipher

3. The Haunted Showboat

4. The Spider Sapphire Mystery

5. Mystery of Crocodile Island

6. The Secret of the Golden Pavilion

7. The Thirteenth Pearl

8. The Mystery of the Fire Dragon

9. The Witch Tree Symbol

10. The Message in the Hollow Oak

11. The Clue of the Black Keys

12. The Secret of the Wooden Lady

13. The Mystery of the Brass-Bound Trunk

14. The Clue of the Whistling Bagpipes

15. The Hidden Window Mystery

16. The Mystery of the 99 Steps

17. The Secret of the Forgotten City

18. The Secret of Mirror Bay

19. The Mysterious Mannequin

a. Turkey

b. Kenya

c. Peru

d. Buenos Aires

e. Hong Kong

f. Boston, Massachusetts

g. Scotland

h. New Orleans, Louisiana

i. Phoenix, Arizona

j. Las Vegas, Nevada

k. Mexico

l. Charlottesville, Virginia

m. France

n. Cooperstown, New York

o. Key Biscayne, Florida

p. Hawaii

q. Japan

r. Lancaster, Pennsylvania

s. Canada

Answers: 1. i, 2. c, 3. h, 4. b, 5. o, 6. p, 7. q, 8. e, 9. r, 10. s, 11. k, 12. f, 13. d, 14. g, 15. l, 16. m, 17. j, 18. n, 19. a

Mysterious Locales Match Game

Nancy Drew stories are set in unique, and often spooky locations that create the perfect atmosphere for mayhem. Suspenseful places are Nancy's cup of tea. Try to match the locale to the mystery!

1. Haunted Turnbull Mansion

2. Heath Castle

3. Moon Lake

4. Ship Cottage

5. Pudding Stone Lodge

6. Pirate's Alley

7. Humphrey's Walnut

8. Black Snake Colony's Cavern

9. Cowboy Outlaw Dirk Valentine's Hideout

10. The Schnitz

a. The Quest of the Missing Map

b. The Clue of the Broken Locket

c. The Witch Tree Symbol

d. The Secret of Red Gate Farm

e. The Hidden Staircase

f. The Secret of Shadow Ranch

g. The Secret of the Old Clock

h. The Ghost of Blackwood Hall

i. The Haunted Showboat

j. The Clue in the Crumbling Wall

Chapter 7

The Style Sleuth: Notes on Nancy's Fashions

Knowing what to wear (and what not to wear) is a valuable skill in business and in pleasure. Always the fashionable sleuth, Nancy has an unerring sense of style, whether she's searching for clues in spooky old mansions or donning a fabulous frock for a country club dance. But no matter how she's dressed, when a mystery presents itself, she's ready—even if that means climbing a ladder late at night in a pair of heels. This style icon loves to keep up with current fashions: She wore a sophisticated golden bob and cloche hat in the 1930s (on the cover of *The Secret of the Old Clock*), looked like a young June Cleaver in the 1950s with her matching dress and handbag (on the cover of *The Ringmaster's Secret*), and sported a polyester pantsuit in the 1970s (on the third cover of *The Clue of the Tapping Heels*). Nancy is known for staying on top of the hottest styles—attracting the admiration and attention of others. In fact if there were best-dressed lists for supersleuths, Nancy would be ranked at the top!

When constant praise for your sleuthing abilities makes you blush, there's no need to stock up on rouge.

The Invisible Intruder

Dress for Success

Nancy is rarely caught looking disheveled—this smartly dressed detective knows that there are always a few minutes before the police arrive to apply fresh lipstick. No matter how messy the mystery or how long she's been tied up, Nancy keeps her composure and her great fashion sense. She has a flair for selecting fabulous frocks and stylish heels that make her look extra lovely—especially for her admirers and special friends. Of course it doesn't hurt that Nancy's father gives her a generous clothing allowance.

A skirt and shorts set makes the perfect outfit for that sudden river swim!

The Haunted Showboat

Always give your hair special attention and wear pretty dresses for the boys!

Mystery of Crocodile Island

While waiting out an overheating car in the desert, it's always refreshing to touch up your lipstick before your rescuers arrive.

The Secret of Shadow Ranch

An old sack tied over your head by a criminal is not a very fashion-forward accessory.

The Spider Sapphire Mystery

Brushing your hair until it gleams can make a sleuth feel extra special about her appearance after an action-packed day of sleuthing.

The Secret of Shadow Ranch

Sometimes you'll look so beautiful in your new frock, that men will drop breakable objects at the sight of you!

The Phantom of Pine Hill

A fashion-conscious sleuth always puts on her robe and slippers before she investigates things in the middle of the night!

The Secret of the Golden Pavilion

13

A revolver might make a nice gumshoe accessory—but not after you fling it into a brook!

The Spider Sapphire Mystery

Make Your Clothes Work for You

Nancy has beauty and brains, which is why she transforms her fashionable frocks and pretty accessories into mystery-solving tools. Nancy is only limited by her imagination: Bright red lipstick is used to write an emergency SOS message, skirt pockets hide treasure maps, and perfume is used in place of smelling salts to wake someone up from a faint. This gumshoe knows that when you're missing the proper disguise or sleuthing tool, you don't panic, you improvise!

A beret is the perfect accessory when you need to conceal a stash of secret clues.

The Clue of the Broken Locket

Dress pockets make nice hiding places for treasure maps in case of lurking purse snatchers.

The Quest of the Missing Map

That locket you wore as a child can make a good substitute for evidence you want to snatch.

The Clue of the Broken Locket

If you're taken prisoner, unobtrusively knock off a button so that your rescuers will be able to better trace your whereabouts.

The Quest of the Missing Map

A skirt can make a nice ruler.

The Witch Tree Symbol

To avoid being spotted by a plane overhead, pull up your sweater to mask your human form while lying on the ground.

The Sky Phantom

A waterproof canvas bag makes a nice sleuth accessory when traveling by canoe.

The Mystery at Lilac Inn

Red lipstick makes a great window SOS when you've been kidnapped and stolen away on a plane!

The Mystery of the Fire Dragon

A smart sleuth keeps an overnight case in the trunk of her car with pajamas, a robe, two changes of clothes, toiletries, and at certain times of the year a bathing suit—in case of sudden adventures.

The Bungalow Mystery

Perfume makes a great stimulant for those who faint!

The Mystery of the 99 Steps

5

Three cheers to the inventor of spike heels when you find yourself locked in a gym and need to break a window to summon help!

Nancy's Mysterious Letter

Match the Outfit to the Sleuthing Situation

Although Nancy was always dressed for success, some of her outfits were more memorable than others. Test your memory by matching the sleuthing outfit to the sleuthing situation.

1. While masquerading as an elderly cleaning lady named Mrs. Frisby, Nancy wore:
   a) A checkered dress with white frilly apron and curly white wig
   b) A light blue frumpy dress, old brown shoes, and gray dusting powder in her hair
   c) A navy overcoat with a dingy gray dress and a pair of house shoes

2. To help blend in and go unrecognized in Japan, Nancy wore this disguise:
   a) Veiled hat, kimono, and long satin overcoat
   b) Kimono, obi, sandals, and black wig
   c) Black wig, kimono, large red fan

3. In order to draw out her ghostly double, Nancy wired pocket-size flashlights to which outfit for a glowing effect:
   a) White evening dress, black wig, white scarf
   b) Black evening dress, blonde wig, and red scarf
   c) Sporty polka-dotted sundress, black wig, and long flowing overcoat

4. To gain entrance to a nursing home run by scammers, Nancy donned which outfit to appear as an elderly patient:
   a) White nurse shoes, tweed overcoat, and empire-waisted navy dress
   b) Gray wig, hospital gown, and hospital booties
   c) Black oxfords, black hat with veil, and long black coat

5. To create a smoke screen while Ned snooped, Nancy played the part of a ghostly hula dancer dressed in:
   a) Hibiscus lei, Hawaiian shirt, and Hawaiian grass skirt
   b) White muumuu and white scarves
   c) White evening gown with mysterious black lei

6. In order to infiltrate a scheming art dealer's shop, Nancy disguised herself as Debbie Lynbrook in which outfit:
   a) Blond wig, large oversized glasses, and an oversized straw hat
   b) Gloves, a large overcoat, a brunette wig, and more mature makeup
   c) A black wig, self-tanning lotion, and horn-rimmed sunglasses

7. In order to thwart masked thieves, Nancy attended a masquerade party in this outfit:
   a) Southern belle gown and cameo pendant necklace with frilly parasol
   b) Spanish señorita red gown and black lace mantilla with matching fan
   c) Sherlock Holmes brown overcoat, plaid scarf and hat, tailored suit, plus telltale pipe

8. While sleuthing for her mail carrier's no-good brother at Emerson College, Nancy wore this outfit:
   a) Raccoon coat, felt brown hat with purple and orange feathers, and a pale yellow evening gown
   b) Leather coat, becoming blue dress with cap sleeves, and a pair of silver heels
   c) Burnt orange camel hair coat, purple beret, and black satin evening frock

Answers: 1. b, 2. b, 3. a, 4. c, 5. b, 6. c, 7. b, 8. a

Chapter 8

Recipe for Adventure: In the Kitchen with Nancy

The recipe for a classic Nancy Drew mystery is simple: Whip up a bit of mystery, add a hefty amount of mayhem, then finish with hearty, home-cooked dinners, delicious picnics, and a sweet treat or two. Like many of us with busy lives, Nancy looks forward to sharing a good meal with friends and family—it's a great way to relax after a stressful day. Nancy has as many culinary talents as she does mystery-solving ones: She can stir up a mouthwatering dessert in minutes or snoop out those off-the-beaten-path restaurants with to-die-for menus. If there's one thing Nancy knows, it's that concentrating on finding thieves and racketeers is tough on an empty stomach!

Mystery or no mystery, a family must eat!

The Secret of the Wooden Lady

Relax with Comfort Food

What's your go-to comfort food—macaroni and cheese, chocolate cake, cheeseburgers? What are those special dishes that put a smile on your face and bring to mind good times with family and friends? Nancy has a long list of favorite comfort foods. Perhaps that's because she and her crime-busting friends seem to regularly find themselves left by a villain to starve! Nancy often heads for a pick-me-up bite after a daunting adventure. It's her well-deserved reward for escaping from a locked closet or being threatened with a nefarious message.

Thick, juicy steaks are a favorite of hard-at-work mystery case lawyers.

The Hidden Staircase

It's nice when a busy sleuth can whip up a delightful dessert like floating island in a pinch!

The Hidden Staircase

When your special friend is coming over, you might get your housekeeper to serve cake and ice cream while wearing a pretty apron and cap.

The Clue in the Diary

After you've been bound and gagged, hot tea can be soothing!

The Clue in the Old Stagecoach

When a firecracker explodes in your aunt's oven, it's a nice gesture to take everyone out to dinner at a fancy French restaurant!

The Mystery of the Fire Dragon

Hot chocolate can take the chill out of any rainy day sleuthing venture.

The Mystery of the Moss-Covered Mansion

Chocolate cake is a great pick-me-up when dealing with a strange case!

The Clue of the Tapping Heels

When your home has been burglarized, it's always a good idea to indulge in a midnight snack of angel food cake and fruit juice!

The Secret of the Golden Pavilion

Eat Well When on the Run

It's tough to eat well on the road, but Nancy has a knack for tracking down quaint tearooms and roadside inns while also chasing criminals on the lam. These restaurants provide a nice break from investigating haunted houses and other spooky situations. Not surprisingly, Nancy usually finds delicious fare and a mystery on the menu! And even when she's engaged in a juicy puzzler, Nancy often finds time for a tasty treat, which is usually an emergency stash of chocolate. The tricksters and scammers are no match for a well-fed sleuth!

Having a housekeeper famous for her picnic lunches is a plus when eating on the go!

The Clue in the Diary

When sleuthing in an orange grove, grab an orange in case you get hungry!

The Mystery of the Moss-Covered Mansion

It's a good idea to carry several chocolate bars in case you get caught in a storm and have to seek shelter.

The Mystery at the Ski Jump

When you snoop in a suspect's hideout and get hungry, help yourself to whatever canned goods you can find.

The Scarlet Slipper Mystery

When your fabulous housekeeper isn't with you on a sleuthing venture, a bakery cake will have to do!

The Clue of the Dancing Puppet

Cocoa and cookies make a great accompaniment to a midnight stakeout!

The Clue of the Tapping Heels

Carrying an emergency package of crackers and a candy bar can be a ray of light to a just-rescued fellow!

The Spider Sapphire Mystery

Don't miss out on an opportunity to dine where they advertise, "Chicken Dinners Are Our Specialty."

The Mystery at Lilac Inn

Watch Your Weight: Diet Advice from Bess

Nancy's first love may be mysteries, but Bess' is food. From chicken sandwiches to ice cream sundaes, Bess always finds something good to eat. That's why Bess is often starting (or cheating on) yet another diet and has come up with some interesting conclusions on weight loss. Although Bess' food philosophy probably won't result in lost pounds, it is good for a laugh. (And laughter does burn calories!)

Eating can be a fattening hobby.

The Secret of Shadow Ranch

Do spinach and grapefruit really make a good substitute for fries and a sundae?

The Whispering Statue

Good food can be a great delight,
increasing plumpness a great worry …

The Sign of the Twisted Candles

When you have a skimpy sandwich for lunch, a big dinner can be like a beautiful dream!

The Message in the Hollow Oak

You can always start your diet over!

Nancy's Mysterious Letter

One should never be ravenous enough to want to eat tacks!

The Mystery at the Ski Jump

Having to choose between two boys can help control your appetite!

The Sky Phantom

Never try to diet in Amish country!

The Witch Tree Symbol

A huge appetite can frighten the boys away!

The Mystery of the Fire Dragon

When an unattractive man offers you ice cream, you can always decline by saying you're on a diet!

Mystery of Crocodile Island

Never remind a dieter that they're on a diet!

The Hidden Window Mystery

"I'll start dieting tomorrow" is a great slogan!

The Clue in the Crossword Cipher

14

TASTY TREATS:
Nancy's Favorite Foods

Nancy has a few dishes she refuses to live without. See if you can uncover the right answers to reveal Nancy's favorites.

1. Nancy is in the mood for this favorite dessert almost as often as she's in the mood for a good mystery:
   a) Lemon chiffon cake
   b) Lemon bars
   c) Lemon meringue pie

2. While sleuthing in mysterious inns, Nancy is sure to order this snack:
   a) Buttered toast and jam
   b) Cinnamon toast
   c) Scones with vanilla curd

3. Nancy learned to make this scrumptious dessert (often studding it with walnuts) from her housekeeper, Hannah Gruen:
   a) Cupcakes
   b) Pecan pie
   c) Chocolate cake

4. Hannah Gruen is known for this continental dish, which might be ruined if she tarries too long:
   a) Pot au chocolat
   b) Soufflé
   c) Napoleon

5. This favorite Drew family meal is as nourishing as it is tasty:
   a) Hamburger
   b) Roast pork tenderloin
   c) Pot roast

6. This tasty dessert was often served as a midnight snack in the Drews' home:
   a) Carrot cake
   b) Angel food cake
   c) Devil's food cake

7. While on the run sleuthing, Nancy and Bess enjoy this tasty delight:
   a) Sundae
   b) Ice cream cone
   c) Popsicle

8. Our supersleuth gets her superstrength from this favorite breakfast:
   a) Waffles
   b) Pancakes
   c) Scrambled eggs

9. The drink of choice for our intrepid sleuth was most often this beverage:
   a) Tea
   b) Coffee
   c) Hot chocolate

10. This lower-calorie yet tasty dessert was enjoyed by Nancy and also served when Bess was on a diet:
    a) Chocolate mousse
    b) Apple snow pudding
    c) Tapioca

Answers: 1. c, 2. b, 3. c, 4. b, 5. c, 6. b, 7. a, 8. a, 9. c, 10. b

Carson Drew's Beloved Beef Pot Roast

After a long day at the office, Nancy's dad, Carson, loves to come home to the aroma of a pot roast cooking on the stove. The vegetables cook along with the meat so all you need are rolls and dessert and the Drew family dinner is done.

Prep: 20 minutes   Cook: 1¾ hours

1	2½- to 3-pound boneless beef chuck pot roast
2	tablespoons cooking oil
¾	cup water
1	tablespoon Worcestershire sauce
1	teaspoon instant beef bouillon granules
1	teaspoon dried basil, crushed
¼	teaspoon salt
12	ounces tiny new potatoes or 2 medium potatoes or sweet potatoes
1	pound carrots or 6 medium parsnips, peeled and cut into 2-inch pieces
2	small onions, cut into wedges
2	stalks celery, bias-sliced into 1-inch pieces
½	cup cold water
¼	cup all-purpose flour
	Black pepper (optional)

Trim fat from meat. In a 4- to 6-quart Dutch oven, brown roast on all sides in hot oil. Drain off fat. Combine the ¾ cup water, the Worcestershire sauce, bouillon granules, basil, and salt. Pour over roast. Bring to boiling; reduce heat. Simmer, covered, for 1 hour.

Meanwhile, if using new potatoes, peel a strip of skin from the center of each. If using medium potatoes or sweet potatoes, peel and quarter. Add potatoes, carrots, onions, and celery to meat. Return to boiling; reduce heat. Simmer, covered, for 45 to 60 minutes more or until tender, adding water if necessary. Transfer meat and vegetables to a platter, reserving juices in Dutch oven. Keep warm.

For gravy, measure juices; skim fat. If necessary, add enough water to juices to equal 1½ cups. Return to Dutch oven. In a small bowl stir the ½ cup cold water into the flour. Stir into juices in pan. Cook and stir over medium heat until thickened and bubbly. Cook and stir for 1 minute more. If desired, season with pepper. Serve gravy with meat and vegetables. Makes 8 to 10 servings.

Hannah's Famous Cheese Soufflé

The Drew family's housekeeper, Hannah, is known for making many delicious dishes. This soufflé is one of her specialties.

Prep: 50 minutes   Bake: 40 minutes   Oven: 350°

- 4 egg yolks
- 4 egg whites
- ¼ cup butter or margarine
- ¼ cup all-purpose flour
- ¼ teaspoon dry mustard
- Dash ground red pepper
- 1 cup milk
- 2 cups shredded cheddar cheese (8 ounces)

Allow the egg yolks and egg whites to stand at room temperature for 30 minutes.

For cheese sauce, in a medium saucepan melt butter; stir in flour, dry mustard, and red pepper. Add milk all at once. Cook and stir over medium heat until thickened and bubbly. Remove from heat. Add cheese, a little at a time, stirring until melted. In a medium bowl beat egg yolks with a fork until combined. Slowly add cheese sauce to egg yolks, stirring constantly. Cool slightly.

In a large mixing bowl beat egg whites with an electric mixer on medium to high speed until stiff peaks form (tips stand straight). Gently fold about 1 cup of the stiffly beaten egg whites into cheese sauce.

Gradually pour cheese sauce over remaining stiffly beaten egg whites, folding to combine. Pour into an ungreased 1½-quart soufflé dish.

Bake in a 350° oven about 40 minutes or until a knife inserted near center comes out clean. Serve immediately. Makes 4 servings.

Nancy's Cinnamon Toast

Nancy and her friends often enjoy an afternoon or evening snack. This cinnamon toast is one of their all-time favorites.

Prep: 15 minutes   Broil: 2 minutes

- ½ cup coarse sugar or granulated sugar
- 1 to 2 teaspoons ground cinnamon
- ⅓ to ½ cup butter, softened
- 1 loaf baguette-style French bread (about 18 inches in length)

Preheat broiler. In a small bowl stir together the sugar and cinnamon; set aside. Cut bread into 18 slices. Spread softened butter on one side of each bread slice. Sprinkle half of the sugar mixture over the buttered bread slices. Place, buttered sides up, on a buttered baking sheet. Broil 4 to 5 inches from heat for 2 to 3 minutes until golden brown. Immediately sprinkle generously with remaining cinnamon sugar. Serve warm. Makes 18 to 24 slices.

The Drew Family's Hot Chocolate

What better way to unwind after a day of sleuthing than with a steaming cup of rich hot chocolate? Nancy and her friends like to have a cup served alongside a slice or two of cinnamon toast.

Start to Finish: 15 minutes

- 2 ounces unsweetened or semisweet chocolate coarsely chopped, or ⅓ cup semisweet chocolate pieces
- ⅓ cup sugar
- 4 cups milk
  Whipped cream or tiny marshmallows (optional)

In a medium saucepan combine unsweetened or semisweet chocolate, sugar, and ½ cup of the milk. Cook and stir over medium heat until mixture just comes to boiling. Stir in remaining milk; heat through. Do not boil.

Remove from heat. If desired, beat milk mixture with a rotary beater until frothy. If desired, top each serving with whipped cream or marshmallows. Makes 6 (about 6-ounce) servings.

Chapter 9

Search for Fun:
Test Your Puzzle-Solving Skills

The Mystery Message

If you've ever tried to decipher exactly what a guy meant when he said, "You're a really nice girl," or "I'll call you soon," then you know all about cracking codes! Certainly reading between the lines is a skill every modern woman needs. But the coded conundrums that Nancy Drew stumbles upon are usually more sinister. In *The Secret of Red Gate Farm*, Nancy breaks a code that leads to the capture of a gang of counterfeiters who is masquerading as a cult named The Black Snake Colony. She also creates her own codes as a way to outwit any villains who may be eavesdropping on her conversations. In *The Secret of the Forgotten City*, she uses a secret code to communicate with her chums while looking for a lost city. In that mystery, the third word in every sentence spoken was the key to unlocking a hidden message. For example, here's a message Bess might send to her mystery-solving friends:

Dear Chums, I am starved. I can spy a meal a mile away. I smell a chocolate cake. You're a villain for making me diet, George!

Can you decode Bess's secret message?

___ ___ ___ ___ ___ ___ ___ ___ ___ ___!

Now it's time to put your mystery-solving skills to the test and decode a message from Nancy that's hidden in the pages of this book. Flip through these pages, and you'll find numbers printed on torn off pieces of paper (like the ones below). On the blank pieces of paper below, write down the numbers in the exact order they appear in the book. (Only one number per piece of paper.)

Decoder Guide:

1=A, 2=B, 3=C, 4=D, 5=E, 6=F, 7=G, 8=H, 9=I, 10=J, 11=K, 12=L, 13=M, 14=N, 15=O, 16=P, 17=Q, 18=R, 19=S, 20=T, 21=U, 22=V, 23=W, 24=X, 25=Y, 26=Z

Now using the decoder guide, write down the letters that correspond to the numbers you wrote above to reveal Nancy's secret message!

__ __ __ __ __ __ __ __ __

__ __ __ __ __ __ __ __ __!

Get Clued In!

Clues are the all-important keys to a detective's mystery-solving success. Luckily for Nancy, clues often magically appear at just the right moment in the mystery-filled world of River Heights. Sometimes baffling, sometimes obvious, these secretive hints show up in old letters, diaries, and ancient relics discovered in creepy attics and hidden spaces. Sometimes these leads are spotted while eavesdropping on or tailing suspects. Whatever the clue, they are truly memorable. Check out the clues below and try to match each one to the right mystery.

1. Crowley clock
2. Phantom launch
3. Black lei
4. Robot
5. Ship's figurehead
6. Peacocks
7. Message in green bottle
8. Paul Revere bell
9. Counterfeit $20 bill
10. Cyclops
11. Sheet music
12. Turkish prayer rug
13. Frog treasure
14. Mah-jongg sets
15. Warwick ship model

a. *The Mystery of the Fire Dragon*
b. *The Secret of the Wooden Lady*
c. *The Mysterious Mannequin*
d. *The Quest of the Missing Map*
e. *The Secret in the Old Attic*
f. *Mystery of the Glowing Eye*
g. *The Secret of the Old Clock*
h. *The Hidden Window Mystery*
i. *The Crooked Banister*
j. *The Clue of the Broken Locket*
k. *The Secret of the Golden Pavilion*
l. *The Mystery of the Tolling Bell*
m. *The Secret of Red Gate Farm*
n. *The Secret of Shadow Ranch*
o. *The Clue of the Black Keys*

Treasure Hunt

Lost treasures, ancient relics, and priceless hidden objects were often the prize Nancy Drew was after while enduring villain foibles and baffling clues. See if you remember these infamous antiquities that Nancy sleuthed for.

1. Frog treasure
2. Captain Smith's treasure
3. Dirk Valentine's treasure
4. Hawaiian King's ceremonial cape
5. Twenty rare Ben Franklin stamps
6. Four gold plates
7. Père François' treasure
8. Curtis family Civil War treasure
9. Precious ruby hidden in figurehead
10. Precious Crystal Cave treasure

a. *The Secret of Shadow Ranch*
b. *The Message in the Hollow Oak*
c. *The Clue of the Broken Locket*
d. *The Clue in the Old Stagecoach*
e. *The Secret of the Forgotten City*
f. *The Clue of the Black Keys*
g. *The Witch Tree Symbol*
h. *The Secret of the Wooden Lady*
i. *The Quest of the Missing Map*
j. *The Secret of the Golden Pavilion*

Hidden Rooms and Secret Drawers

While sleuthing Nancy often stumbled across trapdoors, hidden rooms, and secret drawers full of clues to some exciting mystery. Her powers of observation were put to the test by tapping for hollow spots and manipulating furniture for hidden springs and mechanisms to release their secrets. See if you can remember what Nancy searched for in the following quiz.

1. In *The Whispering Statue* mystery, Nancy gets locked inside ...
   a) A ship cottage
   b) A hollow statue
   c) Her car trunk

2. While searching around for clues in *The Ghost of Blackwood Hall*, Nancy discovers ...
   a) A hidden treasure
   b) A secret elevator to a hidden room
   c) A desk with a warning note inside

3. In *The Hidden Staircase*, Nancy finds a listening post in the back of a ...
   a) Scary mirror
   b) Wardrobe
   c) Cabinet

4. When Nancy spies this under wallpaper, she starts a home renovation project:
   a) Sheet music
   b) Mural of cats
   c) Treasure map

5. The trapdoor that Nancy finds in *The Bungalow Mystery* leads to?
   a) A basement dungeon
   b) A hidden passageway
   c) A child's playroom

6. While solving *The Mystery of the Brass-Bound Trunk* Nancy discovers in a trunk ...
   a) A villain's disguise
   b) Smelly socks
   c) A false bottom

7. While searching for stolen mink pelts in *The Mystery at the Ski Jump*, Nancy discovers them in ...
   a) The hollow of a snowman
   b) A grumpy old hermit's cabin
   c) A snow cave

8. In *The Hidden Window Mystery* Nancy finds a stained glass window behind ...
   a) A section of wallpaper
   b) A brick wall
   c) Another window

9. To cause a sliding panel to open in *The Quest of the Missing Map*, Nancy ...
   a) Clicks her heels twice and does a twirl
   b) Pulls a mysterious book from a shelf
   c) Plays a key on a piano

10. Nancy is surprised by the pesky villain The Crow when he enters through what object on the *Bonny Scott* in *The Secret of the Wooden Lady*?
    a) Ship's figurehead
    b) Extra-large porthole
    c) Wardrobe in captain's cabin

Talk Like Nancy

Though the twists and turns of Nancy Drew mysteries appeal to all generations, the books' language does have a quaint, old-fashioned quality. In the classic books, you'll often stumble upon words and phrases that aren't common today. Take a step back in time with these words and phrases that are part of Nancy's mystery phraseology. Quicker than you can say "Hypers!" you'll be able to decipher what your favorite sleuth and her chums are talking about.

Amateur Detective—*a sleuth who won't take money for her mystery-solving talents. A far more noble (though less lucrative) career path than doing detective work for a fee.*

Bobby Pin—*a hair pin that doubles as a lock pick. This indispensable tool comes in handy when a villain leaves Nancy to starve in a room.*

Chum—*a loyal friend and comrade in mystery. Nancy's favorites are Bess Marvin, George Fayne, and Helen Corning.*

Dreamy—*something fabulous and fun. It's Bess' pet expression.*

Fellows—*comrades. It's the equivalent of the more modern term "guys" as in, "Do you guys (or fellows) want to help me out on a mystery?"*

For Pete's Sake—*an expression of exasperation, often uttered by Ned or George.*

Foul Play—*evil schemes and dangerous tricks cooked up by villains and criminals. The victims of foul play always meet with terrible consequences.*

Frock—*a fashionable dress or other piece of clothing. Versatile and stylish, it's worn by Nancy to fancy dances and while sleuthing in musty attics, chasing suspects, and climbing ladders.*

Ghost—*a shadowy spirit that in Nancy's world is usually revealed to be a fake or the creation of a fraudulent schemer who's trying to buy someone else's property!*

Hunch—*a sneaking suspicion that something isn't quite right. A hunch may be about someone's actions, a mysterious object or situation, or a sinister suspect.*

Hypers!—*an expression of excitement favored by Nancy's best chum George. It's a super-duper substitute for "Wow!" or "Oh my gosh!" It's likely to be used when an important clue turns up or a villain has foiled Nancy in some dastardly way.*

Luncheon—*Bess' favorite time of day, which is also called lunch. In a Nancy Drew mystery, this meal is always something tasty, whether it's eaten at a roadside tearoom or a quaint inn.*

Meddlesome—*describes a bothersome snooper who interferes in the business of others.*

Ninny—*another term for a Silly Goose. Often used by detectives with little patience for scaredy-cats!*

Psychological Moment—*the moment that means life or death (or at least serious injury) for an intrepid sleuth. During these times of impending danger, Nancy either turns into a "wildcat," hopes for rescue by her "special friend," or crosses her fingers that her "chums" received her secret SOS message.*

Roadster—*a spiffy convertible car that, in Nancy's hands, becomes a sleuthmobile.*

Shant—*a contraction of shall not, often replaced today with the more common "won't," also spelled "shan't." Nancy vowed, "I shant go back to that spooky attic without my flashlight."*

more ... Talk Like Nancy

Silly Goose—*someone who is too chicken to sleuth; a term George called Bess.*

Sixth Sense—*intuition that's similar to a hunch. Nancy often followed this gut instinct, especially when a dangerous situation required a quick decision.*

Slip—*thin or slender. Nancy's sleuthing kept her on the go, so she remains a slip of a girl.*

Smoke Screen—*a clever ruse dreamed up to provide an unassuming cover for sleuthing in exciting and exotic places.*

Snoop—*one who pries and meddles into the affairs of others.*

Special Friend—*a boyfriend who patiently waits for a sleuth to shift her focus from mystery to romance. This gentleman has perfect timing, always showing up to rescue his girlfriend when the chips are down.*

Spoilsport—*someone who doesn't want to go along with the group. As a Silly Goose, Bess didn't always want to sleuth with her mystery-loving pals, Nancy, George, and Ned.*

Starved—*hungry and in desperate need of an energy boost for sleuthing. It was no surprise that every new mystery adventure left Bess starving and craving a good snack or a sundae.*

Swell—*stylish and first-rate. Could refer to anything from a delicious luncheon or a pretty frock to a smart new plan to foil the criminals.*

Tart—*to be annoyed or irritated. Nancy and her friends can feel this way when dealing with the offensive manners of dastardly villains, snooty snobs, and ill-mannered tyrants.*

Wanly—*weakly or faintly. After being knocked unconscious, Nancy only has the strength to smile wanly.*

Wildcat—*a fierce person, someone who is a force to be reckoned with. Nancy was often described as a wildcat because of her steely determination to outsmart the criminals or escape a villain's clutches.*